for my mom

who lives good thoughts

To:

From: Kris Brueggen
4/21/97

GOOD THOUGHTS

Written and Illustrated
by
Susan Squellati Florence

The C.R. Gibson Company, Norwalk, CT. 06856

It is good
to know
what we want...

but it is better
to realize
how much we have.

It is good
to hope
that our lives
will make a difference
in the world ...

but it is better
to know
that every day
in every small way
we do make a difference
in the world.

It is important
to make
life happen.

It is also important
to let
life happen.

It does not matter
so much
that we are
young or old.

What matters
so much
is that we are
open or closed.

It is good
to become successful
in the eyes
of the world.

Even better is it
to realize
that true success
is within
and can be seen
by the heart.

It is fulfilling
to be busy
and involved,
with wonderful people,
and important things.

It is also fulfilling
to be alone,
with yourself,
and do nothing.

The dreams we have
for our lives
are important
and some do come true...

but remember always
that the universe
has unknown
and perfect dreams
for us too.

It is good
to spend time
pursuing our ambitions.

It is also good
to take time
and know
that many things
we want to be...
we already are.

It is fortunate
to have material things
that make us happy...

but the most
important things
we will ever have
will be in our hearts.

It is good
to be able
to receive ...

but it is better
to give,
for the mystery
of love is that
when we give
we become full.

It is fortunate
to have a view
of the sun coming up
in the morning.

It is even more fortunate
to feel the sun arise
from within our heart
and shine,
as we begin the new day.

SUSAN FLORENCE

It is wonderful
to have a lovely tree
growing in our yard.

It is even better
to have a tree
growing within...
to give us roots
so that we feel connected
to all that grows
on the Earth,
and to give us boughs
that reach out
into the sky
to remind us
of our place
in the heavens.

It is beautiful
to have flowers
blooming
in the garden.

Even more beautiful
is it to be
a flower blooming ...
to be open
and vulnerable ...
to be letting go,
and offering
our own beauty
to the world.

By Susan Squellati Florence

Friendship Is A Special Place
Babies Take Us On A Special Journey
A Book Of Loving Thoughts
Be All That You Are
The Heart of Christmas
A Gift Of Time
Your Journey
With Friends
Hope Is Real
Good Thoughts
A Wedding Wish